Jim Henson's THE DARK CRYSTAL

TAROT DECK
GUIDEBOOK

TITAN BOOKS
LONDON

CONTENTS

INTRODUCTION • 05
UNDERSTANDING
YOUR DECK • 06

THE MAJOR ARCANA

THE FOOL • 12
I THE MAGICIAN • 14
II THE HIGH PRIESTESS • 16
III THE EMPRESS • 18
IV THE EMPEROR • 20
V THE HIEROPHANT • 22
VI THE LOVERS • 24
VII THE CHARIOT • 26
VIII STRENGTH • 28
IX THE HERMIT • 30
X THE WHEEL OF FORTUNE • 32
XI JUSTICE • 34
XII THE HANGED MAN • 36
XIII DEATH • 38
XIV TEMPERANCE • 40
XV THE DEVIL • 42

XVI THE TOWER • 44
XVII THE STAR • 46
XVIII THE MOON • 48
XIX THE SUN • 50
XX JUDGMENT • 52
XXI THE WORLD • 54

THE MINOR ARCANA

SUIT OF SHARDS • 58
SUIT OF VIALS • 72
SUIT OF STONES • 86
SUIT OF GEMS • 100

TAROT READINGS

DREAMFASTING WITH
YOUR DECK • 116
PREPARING TO READ TAROT • 118
SHAPES OF KINDNESS • 120
"TIME TO MAKE . . . MY MOVE" • 122
WALL OF DESTINY • 124
ABOUT THE AUTHOR • 126
ABOUT THE ILLUSTRATOR • 127

WELCOME TO THE AGE OF WONDER

The art of tarot reading can be as gentle and wise as the Mystics or as blunt and biting as the Skeksis. But no matter the outcome, you will gain a deeper understanding of the world and your path through it. Just as the Crystal of Truth is a symbol of light, healing, and knowledge, the cards in your hands can bring you the same clarity with their stories.

Through stories, we learn compassion, heighten self-awareness, and gain inspiration. The stories told by tarot are no different. Think of this deck as a collection of adventures, lessons, warnings, and characters that will help you on your way.

UNDERSTANDING YOUR TAROT DECK

Traditional tarot decks are made up of 78 cards, divided into the Major and Minor Arcana. The Major Arcana features 22 named cards, beginning with the Fool and ending with the World. These cards represent universal lessons, archetypes, and epochs in your life. The Minor Arcana consists of 56 cards that are divided into four suits, with each suit uniquely focused on emotions, material success, desires and ambitions, and communication. Within the Minor Arcana, you will learn about day-to-day situations, personal interactions, and temporary states of being. In this deck, you will find the following suits:

Shards

Also known as Wands, the Suit of Shards provides advice regarding creativity, inspiration, creation, spirituality, and passion. It can also shed light on volatile behavior, reckless actions, and unfocused energy.

Vials

Also known as Cups, the Suit of Vials provides advice regarding your emotional essence, relationships, healing, and dreaming. As with the essence vials, it can also speak to conflicts that drain your energy.

Stones

Also known as Swords, the Suit of Stones provides advice regarding personal power, logic, ambition, intellect, and communication. Stones can build a house, but they can also be used to tear one down, reflecting the duality of this suit.

Gems

Also known as Pentacles, the Suit of Gems provides advice regarding financial stability, prosperity, and health. All these factors can secure long-term success, but they can also create greed and jealousy.

THE MAJOR ARCANA

THE FOOL

THE FOOL:
Jen

Whether it's prophecy, fate, or free will, the Fool marks the beginning of a meaningful journey. Just as Jen set out to save Thra, you must put down your firca and prepare for adventure.

UPRIGHT: With a sense of purpose making up for his lack of experience, Jen embarks on his quest, ready to see it through. Although you may not be certain that you're up for a challenge, trust yourself—you have everything it takes to succeed!

REVERSED: Don't let your reckless side take over—you may find yourself buried under a rockslide! Keep a cool head, stick to your plan, and remain focused.

I
THE MAGICIAN:
Onica

Allow this Far-Dreamer to inspire you to bring your hopes to life. All it takes is a little magic.

UPRIGHT: Under the influence of the Magician, you can manifest your goals as long as you ignore any distractions and stay dedicated. Unleash your inner Unamoth, and allow it to light your way!

REVERSED: Feeling as though you've lost your wings in a storm? The reversed Magician suggests a disconnect from your higher self, from the passion that once motivated you. Are your goals aligned with your ethics? If not, it may be time to change direction.

THE MAGICIAN

THE HIGH PRIESTESS

II
THE HIGH PRIESTESS: Aughra

Aughra gives a voice to the stones and eyes to the forest. She lives between two worlds, deciphering the secrets of the universe.

UPRIGHT: The High Priestess brings not only a thirst for knowledge, but also a desire to help others learn and grow. Welcome this energy like Aughra. Consider becoming a mentor to others, to share your insight and act as a guide.

REVERSED: When reversed, this can speak to a crack in your heart, much like Aughra's at the Great Division. Don't doubt your knowledge—trust what you know to be true, and don't ignore your intuition.

III
THE EMPRESS:
Kira

The stars are calling, and the Empress invites you to bask in their beauty and abundance.

UPRIGHT: Kira taught the plants and animals around her to speak, relishing her connection with the natural world. Similarly, you are being pulled to relish the beauty around you. This is a great time to indulge your creativity through art, to give nurturing energy to a loved one, or to simply spend time caring for yourself.

REVERSED: Even the brightest stars sometimes hide under the cover of clouds, and this card reversed could find you feeling drained. Don't deny yourself rest. You won't be able to care for others if you don't care for yourself.

THE EMPRESS

THE EMPEROR

IV
THE EMPEROR:
SkekSo the Emperor

There's nothing in the world you can't bend to your will.

UPRIGHT: The first Emperor of the Skeksis has entered your reading, demanding that you summon your own power. This doesn't mean raiding Gelfling villages; it involves owning control over your life, putting yourself first, and getting results—hopefully with more compassion than skekSo!

REVERSED: The reversed Emperor warns of a person or system trying to oppress you. You may be feeling scrutinized, used, and taken advantage of, all because of someone's power trip. Prioritize getting out from under their four arms!

V
THE HIEROPHANT:
SkekZok the Ritual Master

SkekZok is a master of rituals, a keeper of traditions.

UPRIGHT: The Hierophant represents the power of convention, traditions, and ceremony. Certainly, no one should be as ruthless as skekZok, but this card indicates that you may want to consider a tested approach: Stick to what you know to be true and effective instead of exploring a new path.

REVERSED: This symbolizes an opportunity to explore your most authentic self. Are you feeling stifled by convention? Perhaps you're wondering if you've grown past beliefs you once held? If so, it may be time to redefine what you consider sacred.

THE HIEROPHANT

THE LOVERS

VI
THE LOVERS:
Rian and Mira

You don't need to dreamfast to know that this is true love.

UPRIGHT: With the Lovers in your reading, you must decide what you stand for. It takes losing Mira for Rian to realize where his loyalties lie. You are being called to make a similar choice. Will you prioritize love for yourself and others over everything else?

REVERSED: You may be feeling disconnected from your loved ones, suddenly mired in conflict and confusion. Take inspiration from Mira, and remember the first moment that love entered your life. Do you still feel the same way as you did then? Or have circumstances changed? If so, it could be time to move on.

VII
THE CHARIOT:
Gurjin

Let's have an adventure—it'll be great fun!

UPRIGHT: Commandeering your reading faster than skekSil's carriage, the Chariot has set a course for success. Bold Gurjin uses his defiance, determination, and courage to help start the rebellion—his presence is an assurance that you will also triumph, as long as you stay confident and focused.

REVERSED: This may be a good time to reevaluate your plans, especially if you have any doubts about your commitment. Spend some time in the Dream Space to explore whether your mission still resonates with you. If not, it's time to resume your previous post.

THE CHARIOT

VII

VIII

STRENGTH

VIII
STRENGTH:
Fara

Never bow down.

UPRIGHT: When this Maudra soars into action, she reminds you to harness your strength. The most important lesson of Strength is that, even though you may feel nervous, afraid, and angry, you must choose compassion.

REVERSED: In reverse, this card may find you having been plucked out of the air midflight, dashed against the ground, and wondering if you've been defeated. Stand up, dust off your wings, and fortify yourself with the knowledge that mistakes can make you even stronger.

IX
THE HERMIT:
UrSen the Monk

Follow in the footsteps of this mysterious Mystic, and seek quiet solitude.

UPRIGHT: Sometimes you need to take to a cave in the Valley of the Standing Stones and spend a century or so contemplating things. You may have discovered a difficult truth, or maybe you need to process something you've overcome. Give yourself the space to be introspective.

REVERSED: Are the other urRu wondering where you've been? Perhaps it's time to leave your cave and rejoin your community. Although solitude can amplify your inner voice, too much of it can leave you feeling lonely.

THE HERMIT

X

THE WHEEL of FORTUNE

X
THE WHEEL OF FORTUNE:
UrUtt the Weaver

Let the Weaver help you see how the threads of life are connected.

UPRIGHT: Woven into the beautiful coats this Mystic makes are the hopes, dreams, and thoughts of their wearers, creating a masterpiece of their experiences. Like those coats, the Wheel of Fortune is a reminder of life's cyclical nature, calling you to cherish moments of joy because they are temporary. In the same way, know that times of sadness will pass.

REVERSED: You can't escape your fate. The more you struggle against change, the more difficult things will be. Stop fighting, start accepting, and take responsibility for how you want *your* coat to be woven.

XI
JUSTICE:
UrAc the Scribe

The world may be but a dream, but this gentle Mystic pursues truth at every opportunity.

UPRIGHT: In your reading, Justice symbolizes a choice that you face. Before you decide, be sure that your choice is one you can adhere to: You could be called to defend your stance. Write in rays of sunlight, and you will never have to answer to dark doings.

REVERSED: This is a call for accountability. You may be channeling a little more skekOk than urAc when Justice is reversed, but don't despair—this is something you can fix. If you've made a decision you're not proud of, own up to it and do whatever it takes to set things right.

JUSTICE

THE HANGED MAN

XII
THE HANGED MAN:
UrVa the Archer

Your destiny is bringing you to a confrontation that you can no longer avoid.

UPRIGHT: You are experiencing a rare moment when you are privy to a larger plan that the universe has for you. Much like urVa and skekMal do when they are briefly united before urVa's sacrifice, you can see the whole picture and what it requires of you. Before you can move forward, you need to embrace this new perspective and the potential it brings.

REVERSED: You know it's time for your part in a song to be finished, yet you are refusing to take action. It's rare to be completely ready for any transition; this is a reminder to trust yourself, trust the destiny that awaits you, and let go of whatever is holding you in place.

THE MAJOR ARCANA

XIII
DEATH:
Seladon

Resisting change will not prevent the inevitable.

UPRIGHT: A transformation awaits on the horizon, and although it will be difficult, you will emerge a stronger person. When Seladon learns of the Skeksis' betrayal, she bargains, blames others, and lashes out before ultimately accepting the truth. Once you process your loss, you can claim the fuller, brighter future that awaits you.

REVERSED: Refusing to embrace the inevitable truth leaves Seladon wracked with guilt and confusion. Learn from her story, and challenge yourself to welcome the end of antiquated beliefs, harmful relationships, or a toxic environment. You are only delaying your own happiness.

DEATH

TEMPERANCE

XIV
TEMPERANCE:
UrZah the Ritual Guardian

Evil is the disharmony between existences.

UPRIGHT: Let this wise Ritual Guardian influence you with his balanced, thoughtful approach. Temperance advises you to take a diplomatic, inclusive path. How can you blend knowledge, experiences, and the perspectives of everyone around you to reach the best outcome?

REVERSED: When this card is reversed, you are steeped in tension. This can be with your loved ones or even with yourself, if you haven't been living in a way that best supports your health. Seek to balance your life and restore the harmony around you.

XV
THE DEVIL:
The Darkening

The Darkening creeps across the land, affecting all beings, including the mighty Arathim. Such darkness must be confronted and understood.

UPRIGHT: The Devil represents addiction and unhealthy relationships or behaviors. Like the Darkening, the trick of the Devil is to make you think you are at its mercy—but your capacity to heal is much stronger. Seek support, be open about your struggles, and confront the Devil head on.

REVERSED: Denying the existence of the Devil is much like skekSo ignoring the Darkening—eventually, this denial will cause collapse. In reverse, the Devil is asking you to meet your shadow self. It's natural to have darker thoughts, impulses, and urges, but you must be intentional and conscientious about expressing them.

THE DEVIL

THE TOWER

XVI
THE TOWER:
Castle of the Crystal

The Tower prepares you for seismic change that, although difficult, will lead to something magical.

UPRIGHT: Once a beautiful palace, the Castle of the Crystal becomes corroded by the Skeksis' evil agenda. When the Crystal is healed, the decay crumbles, revealing the shining structure within. Similarly, you must prepare to shed something that no longer serves you.

REVERSED: Like the Skeksis, your reality may be built on a facade. Something you have depended on will no longer be there for you: This loss can be alarming, but the Tower encourages you to choose your reaction. Will you give in to rage and anger? Or will you leverage this opportunity to build self-reliance?

XVII
THE STAR:
Deet

The brightest star in the sky north has nothing on you!

UPRIGHT: Whether you're cloaked in glow moss or caked in the dirt of the land, nothing can dull your inner light. Like Deet, you see the beauty around you and experience the world with an open heart and generous spirit, which has led you to this moment! The Star urges you to explore something new: When everything is aligned, seize the opportunity to make your wildest dreams come true.

REVERSED: Even if you've felt yourself darkening, it doesn't mean that your light has been extinguished. You may want to isolate yourself, but stay connected to whatever inspires you and reminds you of your greater purpose.

THE STAR

THE MOON

XVIII

XVIII
THE MOON:
The Three Sisters

Of the three moons called the Three Sisters, the Hidden Moon is the smallest. But does the Hidden Moon truly exist? Or is it the product of an overactive imagination?

UPRIGHT: When the Moon rises in your reading, it's time to separate reality from illusions. You might be able to rectify uncertainty or clear up a sense of confusion by asking enough questions to illuminate the truth.

REVERSED: The Moon is leaving its dark phase, and any fears and self-doubt will fade with it. Be sure to fully explore any residual concerns you have so that they don't manifest as anxiety in the future.

XIX
THE SUN:
Three Suns

Consider this your own personal conjunction, and prepare for an abundance of light, harmony, and joy!

UPRIGHT: The Sun is blasting its healing energy your way, signaling that you have overcome recent challenges. Let this rejuvenate your confidence, optimism, and health! You deserve to bask in this warmth.

REVERSED: When reversed, this indicates a temporary eclipse when the Sun might not be visible but is still present. In this moment of darkness, do not despair—your vitality and positivity will return!

THE SUN

JUDGMENT

XX
JUDGMENT:
Fizzgig

Don't stand in the way of natural order. You are meant for greatness!

UPRIGHT: Fizzgig saves the Shard of the Division, securing his destiny to ascend to something greater. If Judgment appears in your reading, it means that you are on the same trajectory. Use your intuition, and follow your fierce instincts as you approach an upcoming decision.

REVERSED: Everyone has setbacks when they take risks, like being thrown into the shaft of the castle. Don't judge yourself too harshly, and don't let guilt distract you from your path.

XXI
THE WORLD:
Song of Thra

The song that connects all living beings represents the World, the symbol of fulfillment.

UPRIGHT: You have reached the end of your journey. Give yourself time to enjoy what you've accomplished, and look back on everything you've learned. Do so with wonder, and feel the peace of completion.

REVERSED: Even when Aughra can't hear the Song of Thra, she believes that she can find it if she simply listens. You are so close to meeting your goal. Have faith in what you're doing, and know that it's within your reach.

THE WORLD

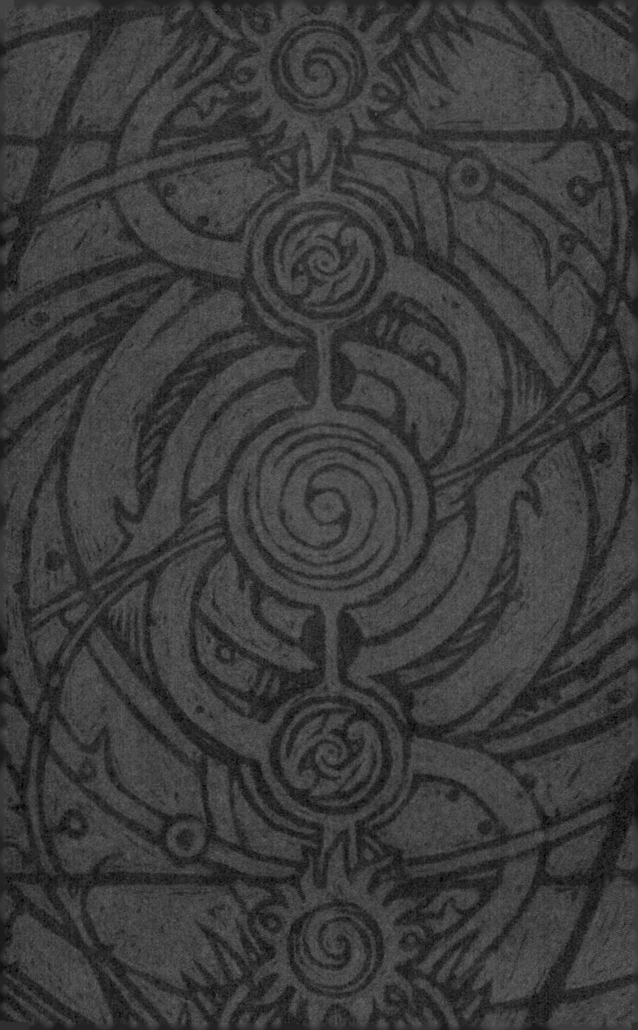

THE MINOR ARCANA

The Suit of Shards

KING OF SHARDS: UrGoh the Wanderer

UPRIGHT: Innovative and quick to inspire action, the King of Shards is a symbol of your rising leadership. Be sure to stay focused on the bigger picture, like urGoh. In his youth, he creates the Dual Glaive, encourages Podlings to fight for their freedom, and provides trusted counsel. He is a planner, not a doer, which allows those around him to shine.

REVERSED: Although your head is filled with visions and ideas, you are speaking in riddles. Those around you are not connecting with your plans, which puts you at risk for being ineffective and losing credibility. Come out of the clouds, anchor your goals in what's realistic, and make sure you're bringing others along *with* you.

QUEEN OF SHARDS: Brea

UPRIGHT: Naturally charismatic and curious, the Queen of Shards encourages you to embrace your power. Be relentless about what you want, whether it's abolishing tithing ceremonies or having access to the entire Vapran library. You inherently know what's right; now you just need to create the world you want to live in.

REVERSED: Using your voice may have landed you in the Order of Lesser Service, but don't let your confidence take a hit. Someone may have tried to steal your essence, but you were meant to thrive—you just need time to recover. Be gentle with yourself, and let trusted friends help you.

KNIGHT OF SHARDS: Thurma

UPRIGHT: This fiery Knight is ready to blaze a path of adventure! This card symbolizes a spark that has caught flame, igniting action and driving you to follow your dreams. Say yes to opportunity, but be sure to have a plan to anchor your passions.

REVERSED: It's time to put on your stone shoes before you burn everything to the ground. While your confidence is high, you may find yourself becoming reckless if you don't slow down and use your energy more intentionally.

THE MINOR ARCANA

PAGE OF SHARDS: Kensho

UPRIGHT: The Page of Shards finds you feeling called toward a bigger purpose—a meaningful quest that will lead to discovering your true gifts. You may not fully understand what's ahead of you, but trust that you won't be alone. Perhaps you'll find a Fireling to light your way.

REVERSED: Don't allow obstacles to prevent you from becoming Lightborn. As a Page, you are still learning your way; not everything you attempt will be successful. Give yourself permission to make mistakes, and try again.

THE SUIT OF SHARDS

ACE OF SHARDS

UPRIGHT: The Ace of Shards assures you that you're ready to begin your own journey. This is a great time to start a new project or pursue an exciting opportunity!

REVERSED: You may feel like you're spending all your time searching for the lost Shard while the world passes you by, but the reversed Ace urges you to be patient. This is likely not the time for you to change course. Focus on the task at hand. The right opportunity *will* come.

II OF SHARDS

UPRIGHT: This card finds you firmly entrenched in research. You are formulating a strategy to bring your inspiration to life, and you may feel pulled toward new experiences, philosophies, and ideas—go with it! Keep an open mind, and use your intuition to guide you.

REVERSED: The reversed II of Shards suggests distraction, a lack of focus, and disconnectedness from your initial goal—perhaps you accidentally drank some powdered null root? It's time to remember why you set out on this journey and to decide what you want to accomplish; otherwise, your energy won't yield any results.

THE SUIT OF SHARDS

III OF SHARDS

UPRIGHT: This card speaks to travel, adventures, and self-discovery. Step out of your comfort zone, and go where you are called!

REVERSED: When reversed, this card indicates a reluctance to leave your comfort zone. Perhaps you see the opportunities available to you, but you just aren't ready for them. Take some time to examine your reluctance. Is fear the source? Perhaps it's an aversion to change? Challenge yourself to say *yes*.

IV OF SHARDS

UPRIGHT: Sometimes a missing shard shifts back into place and suddenly floods your world with a sense of completion. The IV of Shards is the essence of that moment, calling you to revel in the love and security of your community. You may have just completed a difficult task, and you need a break before forging ahead— let yourself have it!

REVERSED: Sometimes a significant moment can be celebrated quietly, without the fanfare of the entire clan joining in. When reversed, this card reminds you to still reward yourself for whatever you've achieved, even if it's with a simple party for one.

THE SUIT OF SHARDS

V OF SHARDS

UPRIGHT: Although a current conflict may feel more stressful than the Stonewood Rebellion, the V of Shards urges you to have some perspective. Conflicting opinions can be an opportunity for you to learn, so keep an open mind and try to understand that what you're experiencing isn't *tension*; it's just *transition*.

REVERSED: The pressure you've been feeling to prove your loyalties, skills, and beliefs has passed. Now it's time to reconnect with anyone you've recently sparred with on the battlefield, leveraging your newfound clarity. Were they really your enemy? Or was the argument a symptom of tension?

THE MINOR ARCANA

VI OF SHARDS

UPRIGHT: The VI of Shards finds you having completed a major milestone, such as replacing the Shard of the Division, and calls you to celebrate. There's still work to be done, but let yourself receive praise, recognition, and support for a job well done.

REVERSED: Even though you feel great about your accomplishments, this card suggests that others aren't recognizing what you've done. Ignore those pudgenubs! Success is determined by your own dreams and goals!

THE SUIT OF SHARDS

VII OF SHARDS

UPRIGHT: As the shards of the Living Crown made their rounds, the Gelfling Maudras knew there was a challenge brewing. Take this card as a warning that you could be called to fight for what you've earned. Don't back down. Advocate for your beliefs and perspective, even if others disagree.

REVERSED: Not every question is a challenge. Even if someone disagrees with you, it's not an attack. The reversed VII of Shards indicates hypersensitivity to feedback and encourages you to listen for well-meaning advice and to tune out negativity.

VIII OF SHARDS

UPRIGHT: Your plan is flying ahead faster than Gelfling wings in the Breath of Thra! Now is the time to take action. Leverage this boosted momentum to propel you toward your goal. Although things are moving quickly, you are prepared to handle the pace.

REVERSED: Have you felt as though you're trying to fly against the current? Your progress may be halted, leaving you impatient and ready to soar. However, you are being delayed for a reason. Try to come up with an alternative route.

IX OF SHARDS

UPRIGHT: No weapon is more effective against the Skeksis than hope. The IX of Shards finds you bruised and beaten, but never broken. You have come so far: Your goal is within reach, and you will be victorious if you can persevere a little longer.

REVERSED: The Skeksis may have come to betray all friendships, without reason and without need, but that doesn't mean that *everyone* is out to harm you. When this card is reversed, it indicates paranoia. You may be wondering if anyone is on your side. Release this anxiety, and remain focused on your journey.

THE MINOR ARCANA

X OF SHARDS

UPRIGHT: The Shard is not easy to carry, nor is it free from danger. Even though this is a temporary state, you may be feeling as though you're fighting Skeksis and dodging attacks, terrified of the responsibility on your shoulders. Remember, the light of the Crystal is for everyone. You *can* ask for help.

REVERSED: Whenever the Crystal is cleansed, it becomes even brighter. What can you remove from your life to restore your shine? This card is giving you permission to purge projects and pursuits from your life that are dulling your light.

THE SUIT OF SHARDS

The Suit of Vials

KING OF VIALS: Landstrider

UPRIGHT: These intuitive creatures perfectly represent the energy of the King of Vials. Partners to the Gelfling, the steadfast Landstriders use their speed and intelligence to defeat their enemies, and they suggest that you do the same. Stay true to your core beliefs, and trust your instincts. They won't lead you astray.

REVERSED: Although you may be focusing on your perceived shortcomings, the reversed King of Vials insists that you summon compassion for yourself. When you're riding, balance is key, and that same balance can be applied to your well-being. Take accountability for the mistakes you've made, but don't forget to acknowledge your wins.

QUEEN OF VIALS: Naia

UPRIGHT: Never one to abandon her people, Naia is the ideal Queen of Vials because of her compassion and caring. Just as Naia is easily able to slip into the Dream Space, this card finds you intuitively navigating emotional spaces, helping those around you understand their feelings and sense of purpose.

REVERSED: When Naia is called to unite the Gelfling clans, she knows it isn't a task that can be done in a day. Give yourself the same grace on your journey. You can't help others if you aren't putting yourself first. When reversed, this card is suggesting that you focus on your needs.

THE SUIT
OF VIALS

KNIGHT OF VIALS: Rek'yr

UPRIGHT: Charming, charismatic, and suave, the Knight of Vials infuses your reading with an appreciation for beauty and a longing for romance. You may be feeling pulled by your heart, with your attention turning toward volunteering, caring for a friend, or even pursuing a crush. Let your emotions lead you, and don't be afraid to let your hands, feet, head, and life belong to what you love.

REVERSED: The reversed Knight finds you, like Rek'yr, not quite ready to explore new territory. You may feel locked into plans you're making, preferring to pour your energy into planning, ideating, and imagining instead of acting. Dreaming is important, but make sure you're being realistic; otherwise, your ideas will never take shape.

THE MINOR ARCANA

PAGE OF VIALS: Lore

UPRIGHT: When Lore awakes from his stasis, his first act is to save others—he is guided by a courageous heart. This card speaks to opening yourself up to new emotional experiences, awakening creativity, engaging in artistic expression, and welcoming deep relationships.

REVERSED: It's time to tell your self-doubt to stand down. Deactivate the negativity, and affirm the rock-solid belief you have in your talent, vision, and voice. If you are feeling unable to express yourself or bring your ideas to life, reconnect with your original inspiration!

ACE OF VIALS

UPRIGHT: Like hearing the Song of Thra for the first time, the Ace of Vials represents a moment when you are deeply in tune with the love, compassion, and creativity that fuels the universe. Be receptive to new relationships, projects, inspiration, and opportunities—the song in your heart is ready to be free.

REVERSED: You may be unintentionally blocking yourself from the connections around you, burying your feelings deeper than a Podling's seeds. If you aren't ready to open up, at least find a way to express yourself so you don't become overwhelmed.

THE MINOR ARCANA

II OF VIALS

UPRIGHT: The II of Vials finds you exploring a new connection. This may be romantic or a deep friendship, but when this card is in your reading, it's a sign that you are forming a relationship that will last through the trine.

REVERSED: When reversed, this card is encouraging you to restore some of your divine essence back to yourself! How can you practice self-love? What can you add to your daily life to nurture your mind, body, and spirit?

III OF VIALS

UPRIGHT: The III of Vials is the ultimate celebration of your clan. It suggests that this is a time to hold your friends close to you. They are part of you, and you are part of each of them. If you have been considering a collaborative project, this is a sign to say yes. Through your bonds, you can create something beautiful.

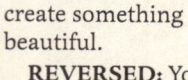

REVERSED: You may find yourself celebrating too much. Are you reveling to avoid responsibilities and relationships? The reversed III of Vials is urging you to seek balance.

THE MINOR ARCANA

IV OF VIALS

UPRIGHT: When the IV of Vials appears in your reading, you are disinterested in the options presented to you. You are not ready to move forward, so make the most of your introspection.

REVERSED: Have you been feeling disappointed with the world around you, struggling to hear the song that connects your heart to the universe? If it's difficult to create, explore, and rejoice in your surroundings, allow yourself solitude. Don't stay away too long, though; your problems won't solve themselves.

THE SUIT OF VIALS

V OF VIALS

UPRIGHT: The V of Vials is a call to release any anger you hold against yourself or others for past actions; it's standing in the way of your growth.

REVERSED: Even if you've made a terrible mistake, you must find a way to process the guilt and let yourself learn from it. Don't keep your feelings hidden. Talk to a trusted friend, and find a way through your pain.

VI OF VIALS

UPRIGHT: Have you been longing for your past? This is an invitation to revisit the places, people, and pastimes of your youth, reflecting with happiness on simpler times. This is a good time to head to your childhood home, call old friends, or even just go outside and play.

REVERSED: A little nostalgia goes a long way! Don't allow your memories of the past to overshadow your present life. Your future has a lot to offer, so stay focused on what's ahead.

THE SUIT OF VIALS

VII OF VIALS

UPRIGHT: You may find yourself presented with choices that seem too good to be true. This is a time for you to think carefully, weigh your options, and make an informed decision.

REVERSED: When reversed, the VII of Vials suggests that you're flitting about, unable to land in one place. You are being encouraged to stay on solid ground, examine what you're looking for, and stop distracting yourself.

VIII OF VIALS

UPRIGHT: The VIII of Vials finds you needing to withdraw, turning your back on an emotionally draining situation. It's time to walk away and channel your energy into your own happiness.

REVERSED: This card symbolizes prioritizing your own voice and following your heart, even if it's difficult. Although the feelings of others are important, you know what's best for yourself.

THE SUIT OF VIALS

IX OF VIALS

UPRIGHT: Consider this card your own moment to meditate under the Great Tree. What do you want to see in your future? Whether it's healing the Dark Crystal or sitting on the Skeksis throne, this is your time to wish for it.

REVERSED: Does it seem as though some of your essence is missing? Perhaps the things you are seeking aren't what will truly fulfill you. Take stock of where you're devoting your time and emotional energy. Is it satisfying? Or do you need to reclaim those parts of yourself?

THE MINOR ARCANA

X OF VIALS

UPRIGHT: You are surrounded by your loved ones, embarking on adventures and strengthening your bonds. Your relationships are in a good place, so be sure to enjoy them! Your own Podling party will carry you through thick and thin.

REVERSED: When reversed, this card finds you wanting two to become one. You are craving harmony, unity, and peace, but you can't seem to reach an understanding. Relationships will always have conflict, so try to accept their natural cycles and stop expecting perfection.

THE SUIT OF VIALS

The Suit of Stones

KING OF STONES: SkekSil the Chamberlain

UPRIGHT: Unlike skekSil, when this King plants stories in the ground, he truly does desire the truth. This is the card of expertise, impartial advice, and honesty—qualities that you are being called to depend on now.

REVERSED: When the King of Stones is reversed, corruption, manipulation, and deceit follow. In your reading, this conveys caution about how you wield your own power or about the potential negative influence of someone you once trusted. Either way, be mindful.

THE MINOR ARCANA

QUEEN OF STONES: Mayrin the All-Maudra

UPRIGHT: When Mayrin learns the truth of the Skeksis, she fights back and attempts to keep the Gelflings safe. Similarly, the Queen of Stones is asking you to use your head instead of your heart, to have clear vision, and to be quick to protect your boundaries.

REVERSED: It may *seem* easier to have no one depending on you, but others can still be impacted by your behavior. Although there is power in independence, you can also face a tendency to be dismissive and aloof. You don't need to be cruel to be unbiased.

THE SUIT OF STONES

KNIGHT OF STONES: Ordon

UPRIGHT: Your leadership continues to impress! Like Ordon, you are ambitious, self-motivated, and driven. The Knight of Stones encourages you to be dedicated but remain open minded. Don't allow narrow focus to overshadow the value of planning your strategy and slowing down to examine how things might play out.

REVERSED: Ordon could have questioned his loyalty to the Skeksis if he had taken the time to examine what he was seeing instead of rushing into battle. Similarly, you will miss critical information if you can't redirect your energy. Give yourself space to think and to challenge your own perceptions. You may be surprised by what you discover.

THE MINOR ARCANA

PAGE OF STONES: Tavra

UPRIGHT: The Page of Stones symbolizes exploration and communication, channeling the adventurous spirit of Princess Tavra. Follow your heart, even if others don't agree with you. But be warned: Achieving your dreams requires thinking in new ways, challenging yourself, and putting in hard work.

REVERSED: When reversed, this Page finds you biting your tongue. Don't hold back from speaking your mind, even if it means disagreeing with someone you care about. Your thoughts are more valuable than your silence.

THE SUIT OF STONES

ACE OF STONES

UPRIGHT: Like the light of the Three Suns piercing the ceiling of Domrak, you are being touched by brilliance. Welcome this enhanced mental state! Prepare for new ideas and inspiration that allows you to realize your potential.

REVERSED: Even the most brilliant suns will have a cloud pass over them. When this card is reversed, you could feel that you aren't ready to share your light with others. Your idea might feel too new or too incomplete, and you might want more time before bringing it into the world. Give yourself time to think it through!

THE MINOR ARCANA

II OF STONES

UPRIGHT: Deep in underground tunnels lies the Breath of Thra, powerful vents that propel you in whatever direction you like. However, you must decide where you're heading. The II of Stones is a card of choice, with neither option feeling extremely clear. Let your intuition guide you; avoiding this decision will only lead to further conflict.

REVERSED: You have reached the dead end of a cave, unable to travel forward. This impasse could be caused by a lack of information, infighting, or a refusal to compromise. The reversed II of Stones is suggesting that you change your perspective, try to see the problem from a different angle, and pursue a new direction.

THE SUIT OF STONES

III OF STONES

UPRIGHT: Although you may wish that your heart was as impenetrable as the hide of a Locksnake, it's essential to experience your feelings. You are grieving, but although the sadness seems overwhelming, it is temporary. The III of Stones suggests that you mourn fully so that you can heal, learn, and gain clarity.

REVERSED: You have found your way through the coils and unlocked the path to healing. This card finds you ready to leave the past behind you, grateful for the insight you are taking away.

THE MINOR ARCANA

IV OF STONES

UPRIGHT: Seek the comfort of a deep Grottan cave, and give in to the solitude your mind is asking for. This card suggests that you are seeking grounding, centering, and a mental reset. Get away from the distractions of everyday life.

REVERSED: Even if you had all the limbs of an Arathim, you still couldn't accomplish everything you're trying to do. Although it's important to be engaged in things you care about, you are taking on too much. It's time for a long overdue break!

THE SUIT OF STONES

V OF STONES

UPRIGHT: Your bonds with others are being tested—are you going to let them be broken? The V of Stones appears when you are embroiled in a conflict that not even an All-Maudra could mediate, and it's up to you to decide whether your point of view is so important that you're willing to end relationships for it. If so, this could change how others see you; think carefully before you act.

REVERSED: Nita and Thurma are challenged to build a Glass Castle to settle their feud. In the end, they compromise and cooperate to create something incredible. The reversed V of Stones is asking you to build your own Glass Castle—you must mend a relationship and end an argument so you can move forward.

VI OF STONES

UPRIGHT: Something is holding you back, and on the other side is an opportunity you've been waiting for. Shed the negativity, and charge ahead.

REVERSED: You might regret moments when you weren't your best self, but you are not a nobody. Leave your past where it belongs, and focus on the good you *can* do. If you don't let yourself move on, you could become resistant to change and miss out on the wonderful experiences life has to offer.

VII OF STONES

UPRIGHT: Are you scheming more deviously than the Chamberlain? When the VII of Stones appears, it suggests that your strategy requires more thought before execution. If you get away with your plans, are you prepared to live with the work required to continue to keep them a secret? Or would it be easier to be up front about what you need?

REVERSED: The weight of a secret that you're carrying has you feeling exhausted. Although you might fear the consequences of your honesty, nothing will restore your sense of freedom like the truth.

THE MINOR ARCANA

VIII OF STONES

UPRIGHT: It can be hard to recognize the light when you've spent your whole life in the dark, but when the VIII of Stones rolls into your reading, it's time to adjust your mindset. Even though you might feel trapped, nothing is holding you in place. You can free yourself and walk away from your current circumstances whenever you like. You just need a shift in perspective.

REVERSED: You are creating a cave of negativity, keeping yourself in a dark place through harsh critiques, unrealistic expectations, and self-doubt. Does your inner voice sound more like a Skeksis than an urSkek? If so, it's time to ease up on yourself.

IX OF STONES

UPRIGHT: When this card appears, your worries seem as deep and endless as the Caves of Grot. Think of the Grottan lullaby, and remind yourself that there is no need to fear and no need to weep. The more attention you give to your anxieties, the more likely you are to manifest the situations you fear.

REVERSED: If your world seems to be caving in, it's time for some overdue daylighting. Seek out the brightest, most supportive loved one you have, and confide in them. Your friends are here to listen, and their perspective may help you feel less like you're trapped underground.

THE MINOR
ARCANA

X OF STONES

UPRIGHT: You may be feeling as though skekZok just stabbed you in the back. The X of Stones is a difficult card because it speaks to a painful ending, but don't lose hope! When this card arrives, it means the worst is over. Soon you will be revived and ready to face the world again—stronger, smarter, and wiser.

REVERSED: If Kira had never looked to the future, Thra would have fallen to pieces. Similarly, you are dwelling on your loss instead of moving forward. The X of Stones is encouraging you to reevaluate your mindset.

The Suit of Gems

KING OF GEMS: SkekShod the Treasurer

UPRIGHT: When this King appears in your reading, prepare to bite your gold coins: Success is imminent. You have found a method of working that suits you, and now you are seeing the benefits of your labor.

REVERSED: This materialistic treasurer values wealth above all else. In reverse, this card warns that you may need to adjust your priorities. Your relationships, well-being, and health will suffer if you can't strike a better balance between professional and personal needs.

QUEEN OF GEMS: Ydra

UPRIGHT: When Ydra finds the Gelfling Kira, she raises Kira as her own daughter, showering her in the warm, maternal love that the Queen of Gems exudes. Independent, financially stable, and practical, this Queen speaks to your ability to take care of your loved ones and yourself.

REVERSED: This reversed card suggests that you could be nurturing others at your own expense. Don't let your essence become drained. Invest more time and energy into taking care of yourself! Your loved ones can fend for themselves while you build up your resources.

THE SUIT OF GEMS

KNIGHT OF GEMS: Hup

UPRIGHT: With this Knight in your reading, you will easily be able to stand and prove the strength of your spoon. Hardworking, ambitious, and focused on his goals, Hup sees himself as a paladin, and no one can change his mind. Let yourself be inspired by his resolve, and stay committed to your journey, even if it can seem like a grind at times.

REVERSED: Unlike other Podlings, Hup is the first to rush into danger, much like the reversed Knight of Gems. You may find yourself craving adventure or a break from routine—let it happen! Give yourself a chance to throw caution to the wind—just be careful not to get airsick.

THE MINOR ARCANA

PAGE OF GEMS: Kylan

UPRIGHT: If you've been hoping for a fresh opportunity or you've felt inspired to start a new project, the Page of Gems assures you that it can be done. Take inspiration from Kylan's openness upon meeting Rian and his readiness to learn how to sword fight. Even though you aren't an expert yet, your excitement will carry you a long way.

REVERSED: Although Kylan's past loss has made it hard for him to move forward at times, he still manages to help defeat the Skeksis. Similarly, you might be feeling like parts of your past are preventing you from advancing, but this is a moment of encouragement to let go of those attachments, learn from your mistakes, and forge ahead.

THE SUIT OF GEMS

ACE OF GEMS

UPRIGHT: Consider this the moment you discover your very own Tomb of Relics! The Ace of Gems foretells an exciting business opportunity, a financial windfall, or the potential for material success. However, don't think that potential alone is enough: This card indicates treasure on the horizon, but your circumstances will still require hard work and dedication.

REVERSED: When reversed, this card suggests that you should not count your relics before they appear. You may be in the planning stages of a potentially lucrative venture, but you're not quite there yet. Keep working, and practice moderation with your budget.

THE MINOR ARCANA

II OF GEMS

UPRIGHT: When this card appears, it signifies that your attention is being pulled in many directions. Even though you are successfully managing all your priorities, you may need to take some time away to focus, recenter, and connect with the work you're doing. Be thoughtful and intentional about how you spend your time.

REVERSED: You may be feeling overcommitted, without enough time to devote to any one thing. Simplify! What are you truly passionate about? Who do you most want to show up for? Let your answers inspire your focus.

III OF GEMS

UPRIGHT: The III of Gems symbolizes teamwork, synergy, and progress toward completing your goal. You're doing the right things and will see results very soon.

REVERSED: This card indicates a sense of disharmony in your team, making you wonder if you'd be better off facing your work alone. Don't dismiss the idea, but see if you can get help from others first.

THE MINOR ARCANA

IV OF GEMS

UPRIGHT: If the IV of Gems has come calling, it's time to examine your need for material goods. Are you being reckless with what you have? Or are you perhaps saving for the future in a way that robs you of your present? Whatever the case, it may be time to revisit your approach.

REVERSED: Are you collecting and keeping material things, without ever being satisfied? This reversal indicates that your desires for stability have crossed the line into rapacity, diminishing your happiness as a result. Financial security is wonderful, but not at the expense of your mental health.

THE SUIT OF GEMS

V OF GEMS

UPRIGHT: It may feel as though the Skeksis have taken too much tithing, but you are richer than you know. Even if you are dealing with a financial or career loss, you have the resources to bounce back. This is a time to ask your loved ones for help and to accept it with gratitude.

REVERSED: Your crops are abundant, your plates are full, and you find yourself surrounded by all the wonders of Thra! When reversed, this card signals an end to a struggle and relief from the stress you've been feeling. Enjoy it!

VI OF GEMS

UPRIGHT: As generous and warm as the Spriton hearth, the VI of Gems is a card of sharing your wealth. Much like the Gelflings, you are naturally generous, offering your goods, wisdom, and efforts with those around you. If you are wondering whether you should be helping someone, this is a sign to extend a hand.

REVERSED: Like the Spriton Festival of the Sour Squash, this reversed card finds you giving to others without receiving anything in return. This is a reminder to fill your own plate first and then help others when you can, but not in a way that deprives you or your family.

THE SUIT
OF GEMS

VII OF GEMS

UPRIGHT: Take inspiration from the Song of the Six Sisters. The sisters assign each Gelfling clan an area of Thra to protect, giving them a long-term project. How can you do the same? This is a great moment to assess your progress so far, look at the big picture, and make sure your output is aligned with your desired outcome.

REVERSED: When your crops aren't growing despite your best efforts, it may be time to rethink your approach. Walking away from a fruitless venture doesn't diminish your hard work; it preserves your energy for something better.

VIII OF GEMS

UPRIGHT: Under the influence of the VIII of Gems, you can embrace a dedication to mastery and invest in expanding your expertise. Keep working on yourself!

REVERSED: This card suggests that you could be holding yourself to a set of unattainable standards.

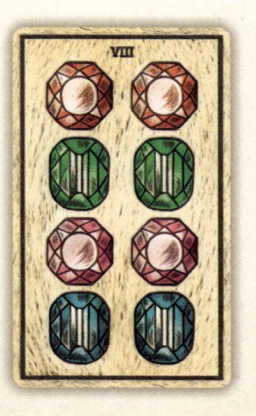

THE SUIT
OF GEMS

IX OF GEMS

UPRIGHT: Like Vapra's royal household, the IX of Gems is a card of luxury, indulgence, and enjoyment of your wealth. You are surrounded by an abundance that you've worked hard to earn, and this is a moment for you to say yes to yourself.

REVERSED: The reversed IX of Gems reminds you to look at the beautiful clothing and jewels of Vapra—perhaps it's time to act your worth? You may be accepting less money for your work or questioning your skills, but you cannot allow doubt to change your self-image.

X OF GEMS

UPRIGHT: There's no need to bite the gold coins around you: The wealth you are experiencing is real. The X of Gems represents accomplishment, finding you successful and celebrating the completion of your project. Consider sharing your gains—both material and experiential—with others! Sharing makes everything better.

REVERSED: Is gold slipping through your claws faster than you can snatch it in your beak? If this resonates with you, it may be time to look at how you're managing your wealth. The X of Gems indicates that you're caught up in a lifestyle that you can't afford. You are never happy with what you have, and your desire for more is not sustainable.

THE SUIT OF GEMS

TAROT
READINGS

Dreamfasting with Your Deck

Before you begin readings, take some time to get to know your cards.

Hold your deck, infusing it with your energy. Close your eyes, and project the feelings and experiences you'd like to gain by learning tarot.

Flip through each card. What impressions do you get from the cards? Which ones speak to you? Consider starting a tarot journal where you can keep track of everything, including your readings. This is a great exercise to start!

Cleanse your deck using whatever process feels most authentic to you. You can use crystals, salt purifying, or smoke cleansing, or you can simply let the deck sit in the light of a full moon. It's important to cleanse the energy of your deck after each reading, so experiment and see which method you enjoy the most.

Create a sacred-to-you space to hold your first reading. This can be your favorite little spot in your bedroom, your kitchen table, or anywhere you feel good energy. The Two Made One spread shown next provides the basis for an excellent first reading and acts as an introduction to your new deck.

Two Made One

Card 1: Which card in this deck will be a valuable teacher for me?
Card 2: What is your advice for me as we begin our relationship?
Card 3: What are your greatest strengths as a deck?
Card 4: How can I get the most out of my relationship with tarot in general?
Card 5: How can I get the most of out of my relationship with this deck in particular?

Preparing to Read Tarot

Before you can begin reading tarot, you must first pose a question. How can I be a better partner or friend? What should I do to advance my career goals? How do I go about saving Thra from the tyrannical clutches of the Skeksis? Tarot can help illuminate a path forward for any situation you may encounter.

Taking a moment to be present and mindful is a great way to begin any tarot reading. Relax your mind, whether that's through meditation or by simply taking a slow and deep breath. Ground yourself through whatever means you feel comfortable with. Then, ask your question and shuffle your deck. If you don't want to bend the cards, you can try an overhand shuffle, or you can simply shuffle them like playing cards. You can also select cards intuitively, by spreading out your deck and picking through it.

Next, draw your cards and arrange them in a tarot spread, which is a specific arrangement for the cards. Read on to learn more!

The Spreads

Shapes of Kindness

Good deeds, no matter their size, can change the world. Try this reading if you are struggling with a challenging situation and need to find compassion.

1. The heart of the conflict

2. The mindset to take in order to bring resolution

3. The mindset of the person you feel at odds with

4. The type of kindness you can demonstrate in order to mend the rift

SHAPES OF KINDNESS

"Time to Make . . . My Move"

Considering an attack on the Castle of the Crystal? Or simply need insight into how you can approach a major life change? Give this spread a try.

1. Your current situation

2. How you see your ideal future

3. The main source of anxiety or fear about this change

4. What you stand to gain from this change

5. What you need to leave behind to embrace your future

6. Obstacles you will face

7. What you need to do to overcome those obstacles

"TIME TO MAKE . . . MY MOVE"

Wall of Destiny

You don't need a prophecy to see what the future might hold—why not use this simple three card reading instead?

1. Your guiding card for the next six months

2. The overarching theme for the next six months

3. The possible outcome of the next six months

1   2   3

WALL OF DESTINY

About the Author

Casey Gilly is the mother of a young goblin, a horror fan, and a comic-book writer. The first two prepared her for the third. Her work includes *Buffy the Last Vampire Slayer*, *My Little Pony: Generations*, and *Star Wars Adventures*, as well as many tarot decks with Insight Editions. She resides in Portland, Oregon, where she divides her time between writing creepy books, hanging out with her cats, and growing tropical plants.

About the Illustrator

Tomás Hijo was born in Spain. He is an illustrator and professor of illustration at the University of Salamanca in Spain. He has illustrated more than seventy books and written ten of them, most of which are related to legends and folklore, including *Tarot del Toro*, a tarot deck inspired by the works of Guillermo del Toro. With printmaking as his technique of choice, his works belong to private collections all around the world, including Guillermo del Toro's and Mike Mignola's. His work has been exhibited in many galleries throughout Europe and the United States. Hijo received the Best Artwork Award from the Tolkien Society in 2015 in recognition of his works about J. R. R. Tolkien's books.

Titan BOOKS

144 Southwark Street
London SE1 0UP
www.titanbooks.com

◼ Find us on Facebook: www.facebook.com/TitanBooks
▸ Follow us on Twitter: @TitanBooks

Jim Henson
THE JIM HENSON COMPANY

OFFICIAL MERCHANDISE. The Dark Crystal is a licensed trademark of The Jim Henson Company, used with permission. The Dark Crystal: Age of Resistance © 2019 Netflix, Inc.

© 1982, 2023 The Jim Henson Company. JIM HENSON's mark & logo, THE DARK CRYSTAL mark & logo, characters and elements are trademarks of The Jim Henson Company. All Rights Reserved. All rights reserved. Published by Insight Editions, Published by Titan Books, London, in 2023.

No part of this publication may be reproduced, stored in a retrieval system, or transmitted, in any form or by any means without the prior written permission of the publisher, nor be otherwise circulated in any form of binding or cover other than that in which it is published and without a similar condition being imposed on the subsequent purchase.

A CIP catalogue record for this title is available from the British Library.
ISBN: 9781803367170

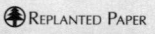

ROOTS of PEACE   REPLANTED PAPER

Insight Editions, in association with Roots of Peace, will plant two trees for each tree used in the manufacturing of this book. Roots of Peace is an internationally renowned humanitarian organization dedicated to eradicating land mines worldwide and converting war-torn lands into productive farms and wildlife habitats. Roots of Peace will plant two million fruit and nut trees in Afghanistan and provide farmers there with the skills and support necessary for sustainable land use.

Manufactured in China by Insight Editions

10 9 8 7 6 5 4 3 2 1